GW01564158

Focus on
English
Year 6
age 10 to 11

Text and illustrations © Hodder & Stoughton Educational

First published 2004
exclusively for WHSmith by
Hodder & Stoughton Educational
338 Euston Road
London NW1 3BH

Impression number   10 9 8 7 6 5 4 3 2
Year   2010 2009 2008 2007 2006 2005

Text: Louis Fidge

Typeset by Servis Filmsetting Ltd, Manchester

Printed and bound in Spain

A CIP record for this book is available from the British Library

ISBN 0 340 88778 8

Parents' notes

How this book can help your child

- This book has been written for children who are between 10 and 11 years old.
- It will support and improve the work they are doing at school whichever English course they use.
- The activities in the book have been carefully written to include the content expected of children at this stage in their development.
- The activities will help prepare your child for the different types of tests that occur in schools.
- The book offers support, development and challenge for all abilities.

Using the book

- There are 24 topics and 4 tests in the book. A test occurs after 6 topics have been completed.
- Each topic need not be completed in one session. Think of it as about a week's work.
- Do give help and encouragement. Completing the activities should not become a chore.
- Do leave out a specific topic until later should your child not have covered its content in school. The book has been written to support the teaching in school, not to pre-empt it.
- Do let your child mark his or her own work under your supervision and correct any careless mistakes he or she might have made.
- When all the tests have been completed let your child fill in the Certificate of Achievement on the opposite page.
- Each double page has a title, explanation of the learning point, practice, extension and challenges.

Topic – the main learning point

Focus – helpful information and tips about the learning point

Practice – straightforward follow-up to the learning point

Extension – uses the learning point in a slightly different way

Challenge – takes the learning point further

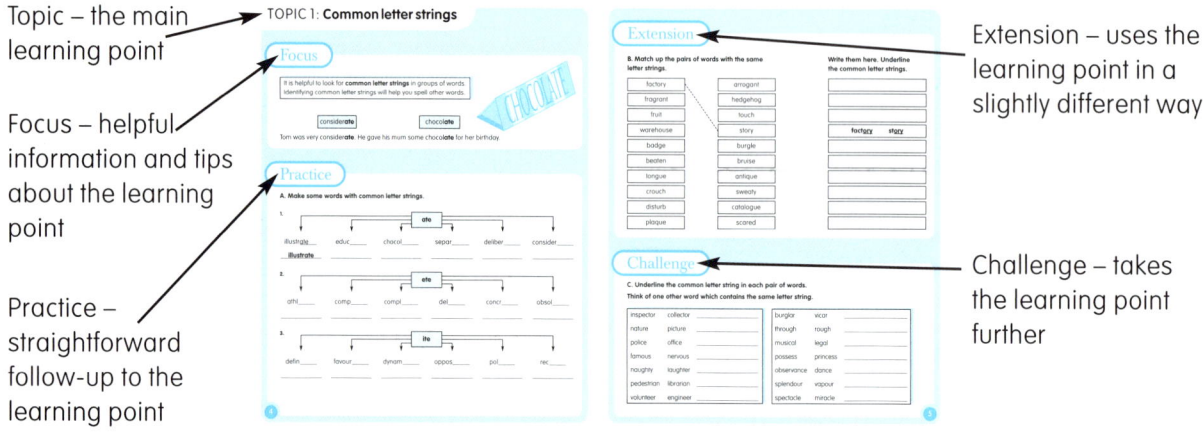

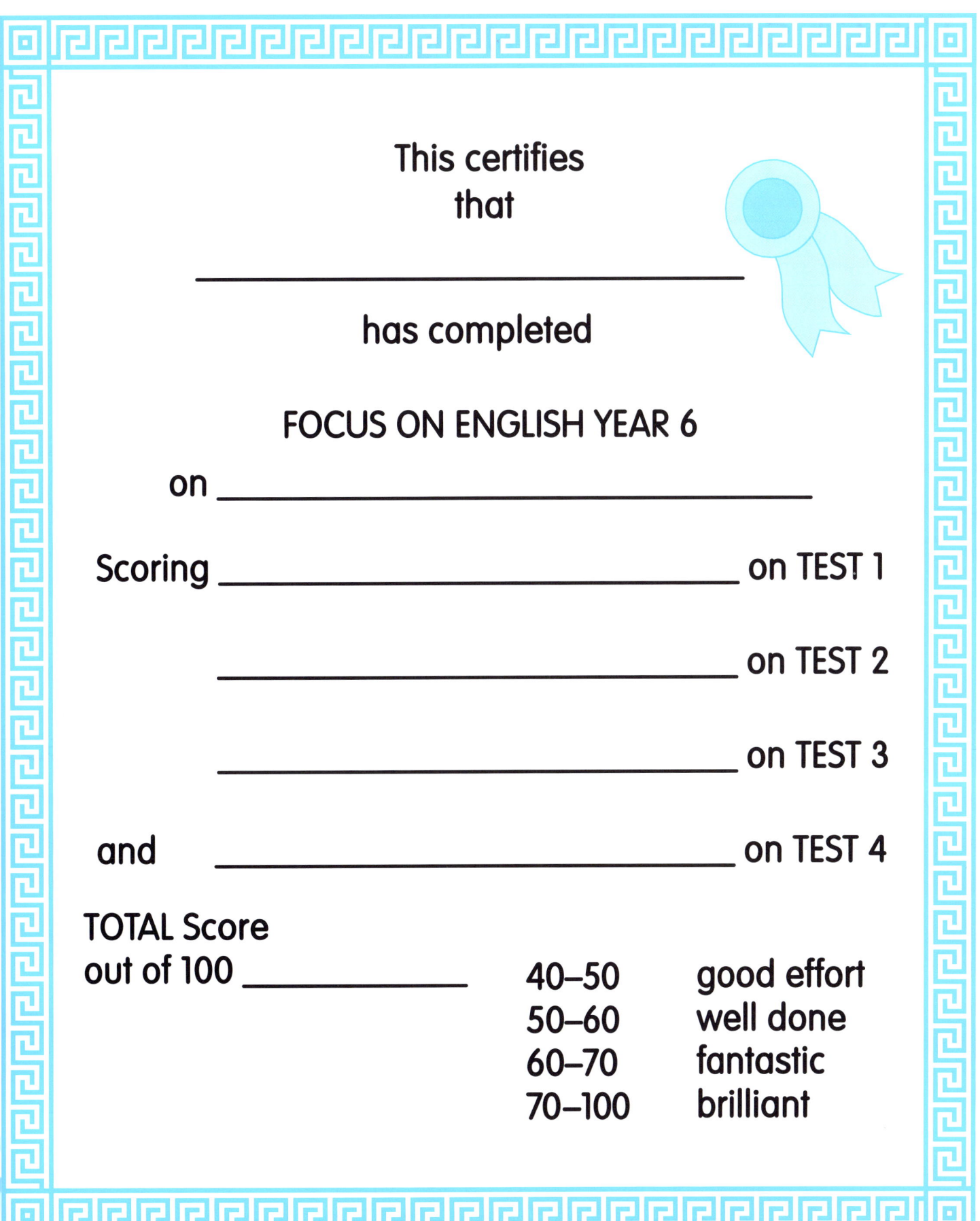

This certifies
that

_____

has completed

FOCUS ON ENGLISH YEAR 6

on _____

Scoring _____ on TEST 1

_____ on TEST 2

_____ on TEST 3

and _____ on TEST 4

TOTAL Score
out of 100 _____

40–50	good effort
50–60	well done
60–70	fantastic
70–100	brilliant

TOPIC 1: Common letter strings

Focus

It is helpful to look for **common letter strings** in groups of words. Identifying common letter strings will help you spell other words.

consider**ate**

chocol**ate**

Tom was very consider**ate**. He gave his mum some chocol**ate** for her birthday.

Practice

A. Make some words with common letter strings.

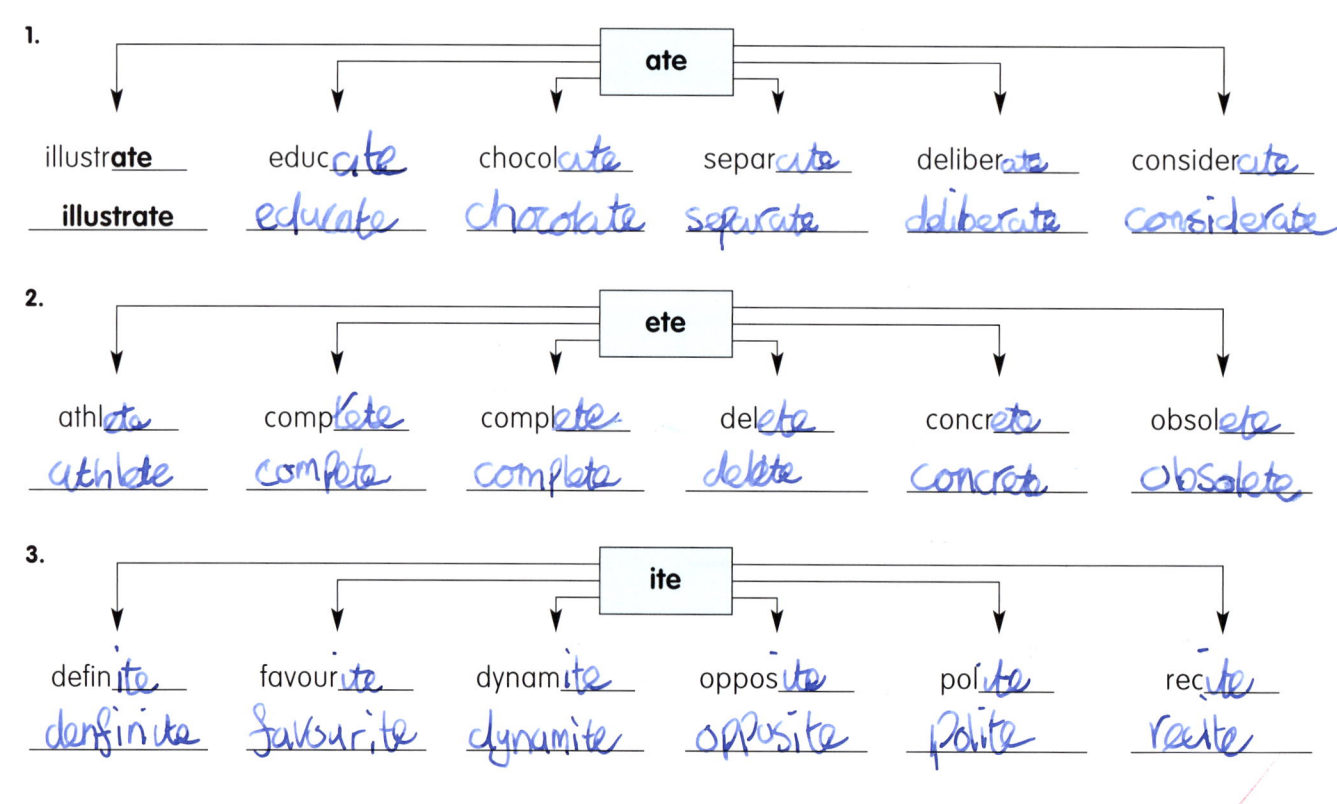

1.

ate

illustr**ate** — illustrate

educ*ate* — educate

chocol*ate* — chocolate

separ*ate* — separate

deliber*ate* — deliberate

consider*ate* — considerate

2.

ete

athl*ete* — athlete

compl*ete* — complete

compl*ete* — complete

del*ete* — delete

concr*ete* — concrete

obsol*ete* — obsolete

3.

ite

defin*ite* — denfinite

favour*ite* — favourite

dynam*ite* — dynamite

oppos*ite* — opposite

pol*ite* — polite

rec*ite* — recite

B. Match up the pairs of words with the same letter strings.

Write them here. Underline the common letter strings.

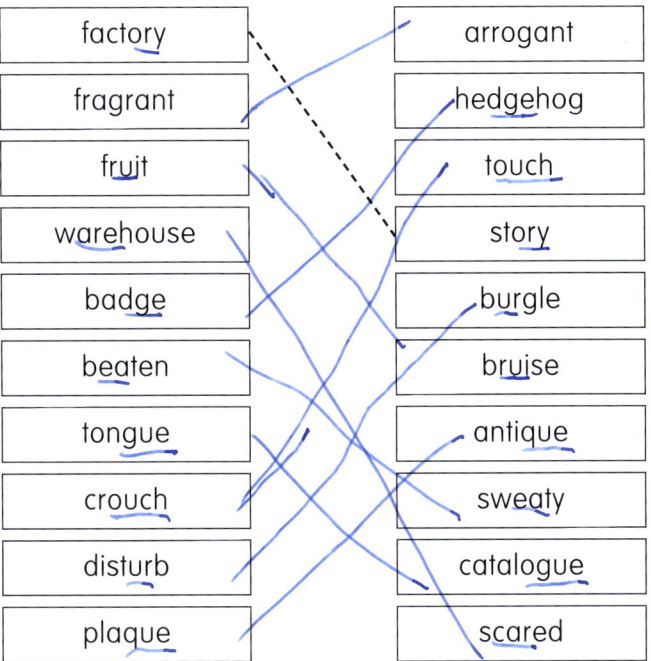

factory	arrogant
fragrant	hedgehog
fruit	touch
warehouse	story
badge	burgle
beaten	bruise
tongue	antique
crouch	sweaty
disturb	catalogue
plaque	scared

fact_ory_   **st_ory_**

C. Underline the common letter string in each pair of words.

Think of one other word which contains the same letter string.

inspector	collector	_____
nature	picture	_____
police	office	_____
famous	nervous	_____
naughty	laughter	_____
pedestrian	librarian	_____
volunteer	engineer	_____

burglar	vicar	_____
through	rough	_____
musical	legal	_____
possess	princess	_____
observance	dance	_____
splendour	vapour	_____
spectacle	miracle	_____

TOPIC 2: **Parts of speech – nouns**

My name is **Leroy**.
I come from **London**.
Can you see **Big Ben**?

a **teacher** in a **library** with a **book**

A butterfly is a thing of **beauty**.

A **common noun** is a **general name** of a **person**, a **place** or a **thing**.

A **proper noun** is the **particular name** of a **person**, a **place** or a **thing**. Proper nouns begin with **capital letters**.

Abstract nouns are names of **thoughts**, **ideas** and **feelings**. You **cannot** touch, taste, see, hear or smell them.

Practice

A. Write the common nouns in the wall in the correct column in the chart.

doctor	dock	orange	astronaut
	moon	hangar	lorry	dentist
cup	bank	carpenter	library
	pencil	church	computer	stadium
plumber	leaf	editor	factory

names of people	names of places	names of things
doctor	dock	orange
astronaut	moon	hangar
carpenter	dentist	lorry
plumber	Bank	cup
editor	library	pencil
	church	computer
	stadium	leaf
	P.factory	

Extension

B. Rewrite these sentences. Punctuate them correctly.

Underline the proper nouns.

1. mount kilimanjaro is the highest mountain in africa
   Mount Kilimanjaro is the highest mountain in Africa.

2. edinburgh is the capital city of scotland
   Edinburgh is the capital city of Scotland.

3. I bought a copy of the daily mirror and the tv times
   I bought a copy of the Daily Mirror and the Tv Times.

4. yesterday was thursday the first day of december
   Yesterday was Thursday the first day of December.

5. sir francis drake was a sailor in the reign of queen elizabeth the first
   Sir Francis Drake was a sailor in the reign of Queen Elizabeth the first

6. we went to the gaumont cinema in luton
   We went to the Gaumont Cinema in Luton.

Challenge

C. Use the abstract nouns in the box to complete the sentences.

fear	strength	poverty
speed	courage	belief

1. The weightlifter seemed to possess enormous Strength

2. The child showed great courage when he had an operation.

3. Many people have no money and live in complete poverty

4. I was filled with fear when I saw the hairy monster.

5. The car was going at such great speed it could not stop in time.

6. It is my belief that one day the world will live in peace.

D. Make up some sentences of your own.
Use these abstract nouns in them.

danger	foolishness	honesty	patience	sadness

_____

_____

_____

_____

_____

TOPIC 3: **Double letters**

Focus

stop – sto**pp**ing	carry	begin – begi**nn**er

Rule 1
In words with **one syllable** containing a **short vowel** in the **middle**, we must **double** the **final consonant** before adding a **suffix beginning** with a **vowel**.

Rule 2
Consonants are often **doubled** after the **first syllable** of a word **if** the first syllable contains a **short vowel** sound.

Rule 3
In words of **more** than **one** syllable, if the **last** syllable contains a **short vowel** and **ends** with a **single consonant**, we must **double** the **final consonant** before adding a **suffix beginning** with a **vowel**.

Practice

A. Fill in as much of the chart as possible.

Make some new words by adding a suffix to all of the words you can.

You will not be able to add every suffix to every word.

root word	+ suffix **er**	+ suffix **est**	+ suffix **ing**	+ suffix **ed**
hop	hopper		hopping	hopped
skip	Skipper		Skipping	Skipped
bat	batter		batting	batted
hum	hummer		humming	hummed
sad	sadder	saddest		
fit	fitter	fittest	fitting	fitted
plan				
jog				
hot				
flat				
big				
ban				
but				
wet				

B. Choose one of these pairs of double letters to complete each word.

| rr | nn | mm | bb | ss |

1. te **rr** or
2. a___ive
3. ba___er
4. ba___ow
5. di___er
6. ri___on
7. le___on
8. me___age
9. flu___y
10. ca___y
11. co___on
12. ma___iage
13. su___er
14. ru___age
15. ra___it
16. bo___ow
17. ha___er
18. bu___ow
19. ca___iage
20. ho___or

C. Now break each word into two syllables.

1. __ter/ror__
2. ____/____
3. ____/____
4. ____/____
5. ____/____
6. ____/____
7. ____/____
8. ____/____
9. ____/____
10. ____/____
11. ____/____
12. ____/____
13. ____/____
14. ____/____
15. ____/____
16. ____/____
17. ____/____
18. ____/____
19. ____/____
20. ____/____

D. Mark these spellings. There are ten mistakes. Correct the words that are wrong.

1. refitted
2. omiting
3. marvelous
4. occurrence
5. labelled
6. deterent
7. rebelion
8. inferred
9. admitted
10. traveler
11. recurring
12. forgoten
13. permiting
14. signaller
15. metalic
16. quarrelled
17. cancellation
18. incuring
19. regretted
20. leveled

TOPIC 4: Parts of speech – verbs

Focus

> **Verbs** may be written in different **tenses**.

> Yesterday I **ate** an apple (**past tense**).
> Now I **am eating** an apple (**present tense**).
> Tomorrow I **will eat** an apple (**future tense**).

> Sometimes we use an **auxiliary** (or **helper**) verb with the main verb.
> The auxiliary verb gives us **information** about the **tense** of the verb.

> I **am** swimming (present tense).
> I **was** swimming (past tense).
> I **will** swim (future tense).

Practice

A. Say what tense the verb is in each of these sentences.

Do it like this: past tense (P)   present tense (Pr)   future tense (F)

1. I am eating my dinner.   (Pr) ✓
2. Yesterday it rained all day.   (P) ✓
3. Will you come shopping?   (F) ✓
4. I am feeling excited.   (Pr) ✓
5. For my birthday I got a bike.   (F) x P
6. We will win the cup next week.   (F) ✓
7. The boy is watching TV.   (Pr) ✓
8. My mum drank her coffee.   (Pr) x P
9. Tom will be eleven next June.   (F) ✓
10. That dog is barking too much.   (Pr) ✓
11. We went home.   (Pr) x P
12. I will have a bath soon.   (F) ✓
13. The Sun is shining.   (Pr) ✓
14. You got all your maths wrong.   (P) ✓
15. Next week I will be in Spain.   (F) ✓
16. At the moment I'm very hot.   (Pr) ✓
17. At midnight the Moon came out.   (P) ✓
18. Sam will bake a cake tonight.   (F) ✓
19. The children are talking noisily.   (Pr) ✓
20. Last week the girl broke her leg.   (F) x P
21. It will be a fine day tomorrow.   (F) ✓
22. The wind blew through the trees.   (Pr) x P

Extension

B. Underline the auxiliary verb in each sentence.
Say if the sentence is written in the past tense (P), present tense (Pr) or future tense (F).

1. Edward **is** drinking. (**Pr**)
2. My mother was humming. (P)
3. I am reading a book. (Pr)
4. The children were playing. (P)
5. I will see you later. (F)
6. I have travelled in a plane. (P)
7. Sarah has climbed the tree. (P)
8. I will try harder tomorrow. (F)
9. My cat is purring. (Pr)
10. The dog was gnawing a bone. (P)
11. William is smiling. (Pr)
12. My friend was swimming. (P)
13. I am doing some homework. (Pr)
14. The children were arguing. (P)
15. I will call for you tomorrow. (F)
16. I have been to Italy. (P)

Challenge

C. One of the auxiliary verbs in the box has been missed out of each sentence.
Mark where you think it should go and write it in.

should	would	could	might

1. If you are tired you *should* go to bed.
2. I *should* buy the video game if I had enough money.
3. I *would* cross the road if it wasn't so busy.
4. I told you that if you practised you *would* get better.
5. If horses had wings they *would* fly!
6. You *should* not stay out in direct sunshine too long.
7. I *could* not eat my dinner because it was cold.
8. I *would* be grateful if you *could* help me.
9. If I buy a ticket I *might* win.
10. *Could* I play with your toy if I promise not to break it?

11

TOPIC 5: **Prefixes**

Focus

A **prefix** is a **group of letters** that is added to the **beginning** of a word. Prefixes often have a **particular meaning**.

bi means **two** as in the word **bi**noculars

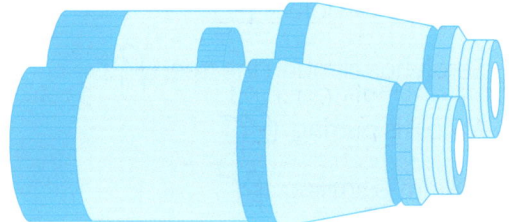

Practice

A. Add the prefix to each word. Write the word you make.

1. auto + mobile = _____

2. bi + lingual = _____

3. dis + agree = _____

4. extra + ordinary = _____

5. il + legal = _____

6. inter + view = _____

7. micro + scope = _____

8. aqua + plane = _____

9. sub + marine = _____

10. super + human = _____

11. pre + historic = _____

12. centi + metre = _____

13. dis + appear = _____

14. bi + cycle = _____

15. sur + plus = _____

16. in + land = _____

17. semi + circle = _____

18. out + do = _____

19. un + well = _____

20. ex + port = _____

Extension

B. Write a definition for each word. Use a dictionary if necessary.

prefix	meaning of prefix	word	definition
in	opposite of	**in**secure	
tri	three	**tri**angle	
semi	half	**semi**circle	
non	not	**non**sense	
post	after, behind	**post**script	
mis	bad, wrong	**mis**behave	
re	again	**re**play	
peri	around	**peri**meter	
under	beneath	**under**current	
with	back	**with**draw	
equi	equal	**equi**lateral	

Challenge

C. Find two words beginning with each prefix. Write what you think the prefix means.
Use a dictionary to help you.

prefix	two words beginning with the prefix	meaning of the prefix
anti	antiseptic antibiotic	against
aero		
geo		
tele		
super		
mono		
auto		
multi		
mini		
uni		
inter		
ex		
fore		

TOPIC 6: **Parts of speech – adjectives**

a **haunted** house

Adjectives are **describing** words. They give us **more information** about **nouns**.

The woman **with the curly hair** sat down.

An **adjectival phrase** does the same job as an **adjective**. It **describes a noun**.

Practice

A. Find and underline the adjectives in the sentences.

1. The weather was <u>sunny</u> and <u>hot</u>.

2. The <u>huge</u> crowd watched a <u>thrilling</u> game.

3. Anna was <u>hungry</u>, Paul was <u>tired</u> and James was <u>thirsty</u>.

4. The <u>old</u> woman lived in a <u>little</u>, <u>thatched</u> cottage.

5. The <u>ancient</u> sailor raised his <u>bony</u> hand.

6. The <u>magnificent</u> butterfly had <u>beautiful</u> patterns on its wings.

7. The <u>first</u> car was a <u>brilliant red</u> colour.

8. The <u>shaggy</u>, <u>black</u> dog was eating a <u>juicy</u> bone.

9. Jenna wore a <u>rough</u>, <u>woollen</u> scarf.

10. The mountaineers were <u>weary</u> and <u>disheartened</u>.

11. The alien spoke in a <u>strange</u>, <u>metallic</u> voice.

12. Some <u>foreign</u> visitors speak <u>little</u> English.

Extension

B. Sort out the adjectives in the wall into four sets.

	scared	huge	sweet	red	amazed	
thin	brown	salty	bored	yellow	short	
	silver	tall	happy	spicy	sour	

adjectives to do with:			
colour	**size**	**feelings**	**taste**
red brown yellow silver	huge thin short tall	scared amazed bored happy	sweet salty spicy sour

C. Think of one more adjective for each set.

Challenge

D. Make up some sentences of your own. Use the following adjectival phrases in your sentences.

with long floppy ears		tired but happy		all slippery and slimy

clean-shaven		long and tangled		out of breath

_____

_____

_____

_____

_____

_____

TEST 1 (Score 1 mark for every correct answer.)

Topic 1

Underline the common letter string in each set of words.

1. factory   history   observatory ✓

2. antique   unique   plaque ✓

3. burglar   vicar   sugar ✓

4. office   mice   twice ✓

Topic 2

Fill in the missing letters in these abstract nouns.

5. knowl**e**dg**e** ✓

6. **e**xpect**a**t**i**on ✓

7. s**u**cc**e**ss ✓

8. th**ou**ght ✓

Topic 3

Choose the correct second syllable from the boxes to complete each word.

bish	ror	nis	tle

9. bat **tle** ✓

10. rub **bish** ✓

11. ter **ror** ✓

12. ten **nis** ✓

16

Topic 4

Say if the verbs in these sentences are in the present (Pr), past (P) or future (F) tense.

13. The sun will shine tomorrow. (F) ✓

14. Dan baked a cake last week. (P) ✓

15. I am too cold. (Pr) ✓

16. My friends will soon be here. (F) ✓

Topic 5

Choose the correct prefix to begin each word.

super	sur	sub	semi

17. _Sur_ face

18. _Sub_ way

19. _Semi_ circle ✓

20. _Super_ market ✓

Topic 6

Write the opposite of each adjective.

21. empty _full_ ✓

22. narrow _wide_ ✓

23. tame _wild_ ✓

24. blunt _sharp_ ✓

Mark the test. Remember to fill in your score on page 3.

Write your score out of 24. [24]

Add a BONUS POINT if you scored 20 or more.

TOTAL SCORE FOR TEST 1 [25]

How did you find the test?
Colour a face

too hard   too easy   about right

TOPIC 7: **Synonyms**

Izzi.

Focus

Synonyms are words with the **same** or **similar** meanings.

conceal		hide

Practice

A. Match up the pairs of synonyms.

strike	start
hurry	broad
begin	hit
narrow	leave
wide	rush
go	thin
call	intelligent
clever	horrible
hard	shout
nasty	difficult

Write them here.

Use a thesaurus. Find one more synonym to go with each pair.

begin start ✓   commence setout ✓

wide broad ✓   large vast ✓

strike hit   **beat**

go leave ✓   exit depart

hurry rush ✓   scurry ✓

thin narrow ✓   lankly ✓

horrible nasty ✓   terrible ✓

clever intelligent ✓   brainy ✓

call shout ✓   yell scram ✓

difficult hard ✓   obscure ✓

good work.

18

Extension

B. Underline the word in each line which has a similar meaning to the word on the left in bold.

Use a thesaurus. Find one more synonym to go with each pair.

1.	**correct**	boastful	sad	<u>right</u>	disgraceful	**accurate**
2.	**adversity**	enemy	misfortune	building	joy	Misfortune
3.	**despise**	clever	scorn	sly	famous	
4.	**hideous**	splendid	ordinary	horrible	gorgeous	
5.	**tranquil**	examine	misfortune	separate	calm	
6.	**sever**	hurry	linger	separate	arrange	
7.	**brink**	edge	summit	slope	top	
8.	**moist**	extreme	damp	pure	vast	
9.	**obstinate**	place	foretell	stubborn	perplex	
10.	**hesitate**	pause	instruct	urge	gasp	
11.	**astonish**	cruel	gentle	surprise	orderly	
12.	**worry**	bloom	fret	charge	cheat	

Challenge

C. Write down as many words as possible which have a similar meaning to the words below. Use a thesaurus to help you.

1.	**say**	exclaim state
2.	**run**	sprint scamper
3.	**nice**	pleasan charming
4.	**big**	large enormous
5.	**walk**	stroll stride
6.	**ask**	
7.	**like**	
8.	**touch**	
9.	**jump**	
10.	**carry**	

TOPIC 8 : **Parts of speech – adverbs**

Focus

An **adverb** tells us more about a **verb**. It **adds meaning** to the verb.
Adverbs often tell us **how** something happened. Many adverbs end in **ly**.

Cara stroked the cat **gently**.

Practice

A. Think of a suitable adverb ending in ly **to complete each sentence.**

1. I walked _____ to school because I was late.

2. I dressed _____ to go to the party.

3. The car braked _____ when the child ran into the road.

4. I shouted _____ when I won the prize.

5. The dog growled _____ at the stranger.

6. We all laughed _____ at the joke.

7. I stepped _____ on each stepping stone across the river.

8. I cried _____ when my pet cat died.

9. We listened _____ to our teacher's instructions.

10. Last night it rained _____.

11. Mr Hills waited _____ at the bus stop.

12. The actors performed _____ in the play.

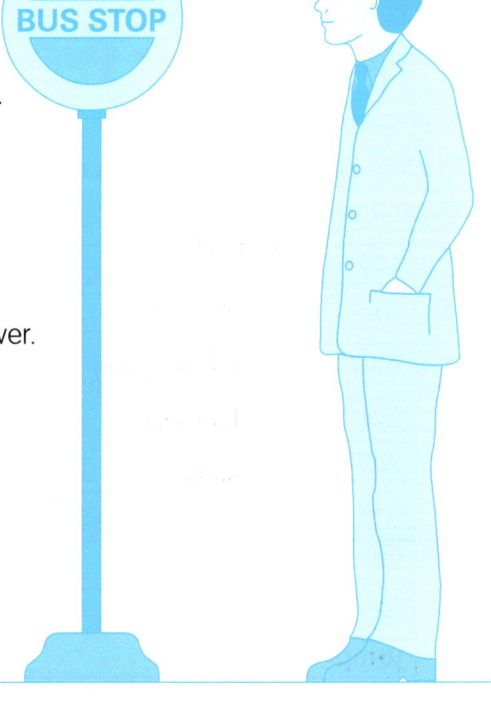

Extension

B. Circle the odd one out in each set of adverbs.

1. secretly	furtively	quietly	sneakily
2. keenly	usually	eagerly	enthusiastically
3. bravely	courageously	happily	valiantly
4. carefully	warily	awkwardly	cautiously
5. shyly	angrily	timidly	bashfully
6. fairly	cunningly	slyly	craftily
7. sadly	tiredly	wearily	exhaustedly
8. foolishly	equally	stupidly	senselessly
9. swiftly	quickly	speedily	pleasantly
10. nervously	cleverly	worriedly	anxiously

Challenge

C. Rewrite the sentences. Change the adverb in each one to make it mean the opposite.

1. I sighed happily. _____

2. The children spoke noisily. _____

3. I put my clothes tidily on the chair. _____

4. I did all my sums incorrectly. _____

5. The nurse treated me gently. _____

6. The river flowed rapidly. _____

7. The boy spoke politely. _____

8. I did my writing carelessly. _____

9. The thief answered honestly. _____

10. The child spoke clearly. _____

TOPIC 9: **Common sayings**

Focus

> **Some common sayings** have been around for **a long time**.
> They are sometimes **hard to understand**!

It's raining cats and dogs.	←	This really means: It's raining hard!

Practice

A. Match the beginnings and endings of these well-known sayings.

The early bird	are soon parted.
New brooms	run deep.
A fool and his money	deserves another.
No news	catches the worm.
Practice	sweep clean.
Great minds	blames his tools.
Still waters	makes perfect.
A friend in need	keeps the doctor away.
One good turn	is a friend indeed.
Early to bed	is good news.
A bad workman	early to rise.
An apple a day	think alike.

Extension

B. Match up each saying with its correct meaning.

to put the cart before the horse	to act unfairly
to sit on the fence	to overdo work and play
to hang your head	to refuse to take sides in an argument
to strike while the iron is hot	to be ashamed of yourself
to face the music	to do things the wrong way round
to hit below the belt	to be exactly right
to hit the nail on the head	to take punishment without complaint
to kick up a dust	to act while conditions are favourable
to hold one's tongue	to create a row
to burn the candle at both ends	to keep silent

Challenge

C. Say what you think we are meant to learn from these common sayings.

1.	Don't put all your eggs in one basket.
2.	A rolling stone gathers no moss.
3.	One man's meat is another man's poison.
4.	Make hay while the sun shines.
5.	Empty vessels make most noise.
6.	Cut your coat according to your cloth.
7.	Birds of a feather flock together.
8.	Every cloud has a silver lining.
9.	Out of the frying pan into the fire.
10.	Don't count your chickens before they are hatched.

TOPIC 10: **Parts of speech – pronouns**

Focus

A **pronoun** is a word that **takes the place of a noun**.

Harry got told off when **he** was late.

Pronouns may be either **singular** or **plural**.
A piece of writing may be written in:
the **1st person** when it is about **ourselves**, e.g. **I** (singular), **we** (plural)
the **2nd person** when it is about **you**, e.g. **you** (may be singular or plural)
the **3rd person** when it is about **others**, e.g. **he, she, it** (singular), **they** (plural)

Practice

A. Write who **or** what **each underlined pronoun stands for.**

1. Sophie has a cat. She (_____) is always stroking it (_____).

2. Tom wanted the trainers but they (_____) were too dear for him (_____).

3. "Are you (_____) ready?" Mrs Barnes asked the twins.

4. When the baby saw Ben, he (_____) made her (_____) laugh.

5. The children went to call for their friends but they (_____) were not in.

6. "I (_____) love loud music," Jenny said.

B. Choose the correct pronoun to complete each sentence.

1. "You can't have that pen. It's _____ (my/mine)," Cara shouted at Sam.

2. The boy lost _____ (her/his) book on the way to school.

3. "Are these _____ (your/our) sandwiches?" the teacher asked Amy.

4. This bag has no name on it but I'm sure it's _____ (your/yours).

5. The crocodile opened_____ (my/its) huge mouth.

6. I asked the children if the toys were _____ (hers/theirs).

Extension

C. Say in which person the underlined pronouns are written.

1. <u>I</u> read a book. (___**1st person singular**___)

2. <u>He</u> rides a bike. (_____)

3. <u>They</u> are happy. (_____)

4. <u>She</u> has a bag. (_____)

5. <u>It</u> is going fast. (_____)

6. <u>We</u> are at home. (_____)

7. "What are <u>you</u> doing?" the teacher asked Ben.   (_____)

8. "Where are <u>you</u> going?" the man asked the boys.   (_____)

D. Fill in the pronoun that has been missed out of each sentence.

1. Last night, _____ began to snow. (3rd person singular)

2. Will _____ pass me that newspaper, please? (2nd person singular)

3. _____ love playing computer games. (1st person singular)

4. Sam called for Emma and then _____ went to the park. (3rd person plural)

5. Anna is untidy. _____ leaves her clothes everywhere. (3rd person singular)

6. Ben put on his boots. _____ ran onto the football pitch. (3rd person singular)

Challenge

E. This story is written in the 3rd person. Underline all the pronouns in it.

Sam did not like the woods at night. He could hear strange sounds all around. He decided to get out of there as quickly as possible. He began to run. Just then Sam heard an even louder noise. He stopped. He peered into the darkness but he could see nothing. Soon Sam was out of the woods. He was safe at last!

F. Now write the story in the 1st person as if you were Sam. Do it like this:

<u>**I did not like the woods at night.**</u> _____

_____

_____

_____

_____

_____

TOPIC 11: **Suffixes**

A **suffix** is a **group of letters** that is added to the **end** of a word.
A suffix may change the **job** the word does.

| angel (noun) | | angel**ic** (adjective) |

Practice

A. Make these nouns into adjectives ending in ous.
Take care with the spelling!

Set 1

noun	adjective
danger	dangerous
peril	
mountain	
poison	

Set 2

noun	adjective
fame	famous
nerve	
adventure	
ridicule	

Set 3

noun	adjective
mystery	mysterious
fury	
luxury	
glory	

B. Complete each sentence saying what you noticed about each set.

Set 1. The spelling of the noun remained the _____ when **ous** was added.

Set 2. In this set of words, the letter ___ at the end of the words was _____ before the suffix **ous** was added.

Set 3. In the words in this set, the letter ___ was changed to ___ before the suffix **ous** was added.

Extension

C. Underline the suffix in each adjective. Write the noun from which each adjective comes. Take care! The spelling of the noun will need altering a little.

adjective	noun
beauti<u>ful</u>	beauty
hungry	_____
responsible	_____
wondrous	_____
argumentative	_____
glorious	_____
circular	_____
fortunate	_____

adjective	noun
roguish	_____
awful	_____
Portuguese	_____
gigantic	_____
memorable	_____
metallic	_____
furry	_____
natural	_____

Challenge

D. Add one of the suffixes in the box to each noun to change it into an adjective.

Sometimes you may have to change the spelling of the noun slightly to do so.

ous	y	ic	ful	ive	ian	al

noun	adjective
nation	national
adventure	_____
water	_____
athlete	_____
force	_____
secret	_____
tragedy	_____
victory	_____

noun	adjective
smoke	_____
plenty	_____
centre	_____
Canada	_____
response	_____
fame	_____
poet	_____
Brazil	_____

TOPIC 12 : **Parts of speech – prepositions**

Focus

A **preposition** is a word that shows the **relationship** of one thing to another. Prepositions often tell us about **position**.

There were lots of apples **on** the tree.

Practice

A. Here are some common prepositions.

above	across	behind	below	between	down
from	near	over	through	under	upon

Write the prepositions with:

four letters	_____ _____ _____ _____ _____

five letters	_____ _____ _____

six letters	_____ _____

seven letters	_____ _____

B. Fill in the missing vowels in these prepositions.

1. _b_v_

2. _cr_ss

3. b_h_nd

4. b_l_w

5. b_tw_ _n

6. d_wn

7. fr_m

8. n_ _r

9. _v_r

10. thr_ _gh

11. _nd_r

12. _p_n

Extension

C. Match up the pairs of prepositions with opposite meanings.

on	under
above	without
over	before
down	off
inside	to
with	below
from	up
after	outside

D. Find and underline a preposition in each of these words.

1. thunder
2. supplier
3. rainbow
4. office
5. hovered
6. pond
7. Dover
8. rafters

Challenge

E. Think of a suitable preposition to complete each of the following phrases.

1. according _____

2. conflict _____

3. to be good _____

4. to apply _____

5. to be angry _____

6. to get the blame _____

7. to shrink _____

8. to be ashamed _____

9. to aim _____

10. to despair _____

11. in defiance _____

12. to be disgusted _____

13. to be conscious _____

14. to have a dislike _____

15. to fill _____

16. to wait _____

17. to write _____

18. to suffer _____

19. to meddle _____

20. opposite _____

21. guilty _____

TEST 2 (Score 1 mark for every correct answer.)

Topic 7

(Questions 1–4) Match up the words in Set A to the words in Set B with similar meanings.

Set A	clever	peaceful	strike	commence

Set B	calm	intelligent	start	hit

Topic 8

Match up the adverbs with opposite meanings.

5. gently   rudely

6. rapidly   roughly

7. politely   sadly

8. merrily   slowly

Topic 9

Choose the correct word from the box to complete each well-known saying.

bird	vessels	broom	minds

9. Empty _____ make most noise.

10. Great _____ think alike.

11. The early _____ catches the worm.

12. A new _____ sweeps clean.

Topic 10

Say who **or** what **each underlined pronoun stands for.**

13. "What are you (_____) doing?" the teacher asked Ben.

14. The wind blew so hard it (_____) blew a tree down.

15. "We (_____) love singing," the twins said.

16. Sam called for Emma and Amy but they (_____) weren't in.

Topic 11

Add the suffixes to the nouns to make some adjectives.

Spell the words you make correctly.

17. beauty + ful = _____

18. adventure + ous = _____

19. response + ible = _____

20. fortune + ate = _____

Topic 12

Fill in the missing vowels to make some prepositions.

21. _b_v_

22. _ _t s_d_

23. _v_r

24. b_n_ _th

Mark the test. Remember to fill in your score on page 3.

Write your score out of 24.

Add a BONUS POINT if you scored 20 or more.

TOTAL SCORE FOR TEST 2

How did you find the test?

Colour a face

too hard   too easy   about right

TOPIC 13 : **Word origins**

English is **not** just **one language**. Over the years, we have incorporated words from many other languages.

Ballet is really a French word.

Practice

We have "borrowed" all these et **words from French.**

duvet	trumpet	banquet	sachet	ballet
scarlet	bracket	bouquet	cabaret	blanket

A. Use the words to complete this chart.

et sounds like **ay** in **day**	et sounds like **et** in **wet**

B. Now use the words to complete these sentences.

1. A ___duvet___ is a bed covering.

2. _____ is a bright red colour.

3. A _____ is a bunch of flowers.

4. _____ is a type of dance.

5. A _____ is a small packet.

6. A _____ holds up a shelf.

7. A _____ is a brass instrument.

8. A _____ is a special feast.

9. A _____ goes over a sheet.

10. A _____ is a variety of different entertainments.

C. Below are some Italian and Spanish words we have "borrowed". The Italian words are all to do with music and the arts. The Spanish words are all to do with activities of old Spanish explorers. Sort the words into sets.

piano	tomato	banana
ballerina	potato	opera
galleon	chocolate	hurricane
soprano	violin	concert

words from Italian	words from Spanish

D. These words come from India. Write what each word means.

pyjamas _____

verandah _____

shampoo _____

bungalow _____

Challenge

E. A lot of our words originate from Greek.

Write which English word you think we get from each Greek root word.

biology
dialogue
grammar
optician
astrology
television
metre
cosmetic
microphone
politics
sphere
pathetic

Greek root word	meaning	English word
aster	star	
bios	life	
kosmos	beauty	
logos	word/speech	
metron	a measure	
pathos	suffering	
phone	sound	
polis	city	
gramma	letter/thing written	
tele	from afar	
sphaira	globe/ball	
optikus	to do with sight	

33

TOPIC 14: **Word order**

Sometimes we can **change the order of words** within a sentence **without changing the meaning** of the sentence.

| Last week I caught a cold. | I caught a cold last week. |

Practice

A. Underline the adverb in each sentence. Rewrite each sentence, beginning with the adverb.

1. The old car rattled <u>noisily</u> along the street.

   Noisily, the old car rattled along the street.

2. Anna quickly did her homework.

3. The thief crept quietly around the house.

4. Sam dribbled past his opponent skilfully.

5. The wind got up suddenly.

6. I did my best writing neatly in my book.

7. Tom smiled at his old aunt sweetly.

8. The carthorse plodded tiredly up the hill.

9. I gasped breathlessly, "I can't go on!"

10. Tara accepted the winning cup graciously.

Extension

B. Underline the conjunction in each sentence. Rewrite each sentence, beginning with the conjunction.

1. We will go out <u>if</u> the weather is fine.

   If the weather is fine, we will go out.

2. Jack read a book while I ate my tea.

3. Mum is not happy unless we are good.

4. The crowd cheered as the band played.

5. We can go out when our uncle arrives.

6. I would buy a car if I won a lot of money.

7. The bell rang while I was in the bath.

8. You can't see unless you open your eyes!

9. I limped badly as I walked along.

10. A child was hurt when the car crashed.

Challenge

C. Find a way of rearranging the words in each sentence without altering its meaning.

1. We went to France on holiday.

2. Tom had a drink when he stopped.

3. The owl hunted for prey at night.

4. The car stopped suddenly.

5. The girl looked shyly at the boy.

6. The woman laughed as she came in.

7. The bear appeared out of the woods.

8. A child sat under the old oak tree.

9. Shut the door, please.

10. There were six apples in the bag.

TOPIC 15: **Spelling rules**

Focus

> It was a rel**ie**f when the th**ie**f who robbed my n**ie**ce rec**ei**ved a long jail sentence.

> A **useful rule** to remember is:
> **i** (when it sounds like **ee**) comes **before e** but **not after c**.

Practice

A. Make these words:

1.

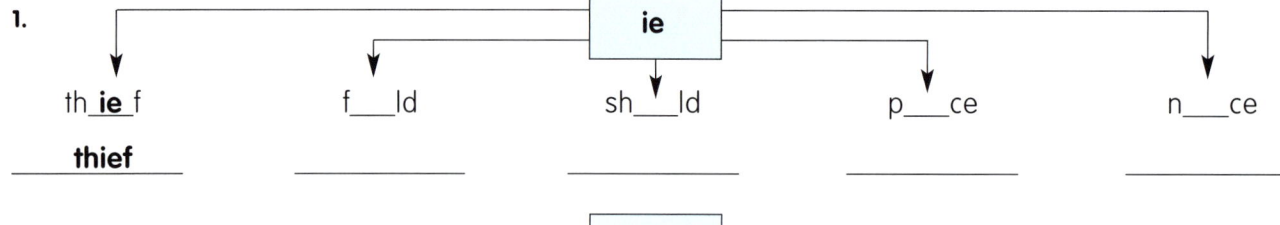

th_**ie**_f   f___ld   sh___ld   p___ce   n___ce

_____**thief**_____   _____   _____   _____   _____

2.

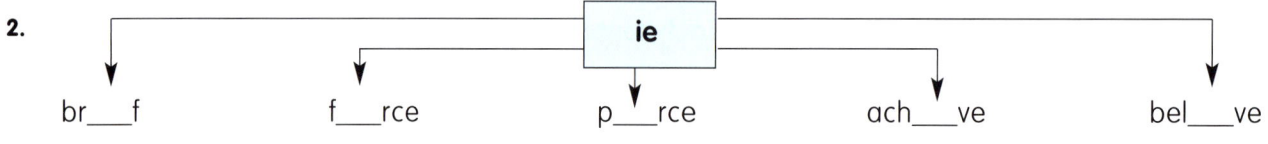

br___f   f___rce   p___rce   ach___ve   bel___ve

_____   _____   _____   _____   _____

B. Choose ie or ei to complete each word. Remember the rule!

1. shr **ie** k ___**shriek**___	2. rec___ve _____	3. pr___st _____	4. c___ling _____	5. misch___f _____
6. p___ce _____	7. dec___ve _____	8. sh___ld _____	9. rel___f _____	10. conc___t _____
11. y___ld _____	12. bel___ve _____	13. rec___pt _____	14. gr___f _____	15. perc___ve _____

Extension

C. Here's another useful rule to remember:

> When adding a suffix beginning with **a** or **o** after a "soft" **c** or **g**, always retain the silent **e** to keep the **c** or **g** "soft" e.g. notice – noticeable; outrage – outrageous.

There are six mistakes in the words below. Follow the rule above.

Mark the spellings and correct any mistakes.

1. traceable ☐	2. noticable ☐	3. changable ☐	4. manageable ☐
5. couragous ☐	6. advantagous ☐	7. peaceable ☐	8. serviceable ☐
9. chargeable ☐	10. enforcable ☐	11. replaceable ☐	12. outragous ☐

Challenge

D. Complete the table of rules to help you remember about silent letters.

Use a dictionary and add more examples for each rule.

silent letter	rule	examples
b	often preceded by **m** at the end of words	com**b**
b	sometimes followed by **t**	dou**b**t
c	often preceded by **s**	s**c**issors
g	often followed by **n**	**g**nat
h	sometimes preceded by **g** or **r**	g**h**astly, r**h**yme
h	sometimes **h** comes at the beginning of a word and is followed by **o**	**h**onest
k	often followed by **n**	**k**now
l	often followed by **k** or **m**	fo**l**k, pa**l**m
n	usually preceded by **m**	colum**n**
p	often followed by **n** or **s**	**p**neumonia, **p**salm
t	often preceded by **s**	whis**t**le

TOPIC 16: **Active and passive verbs**

The girl **slammed** the door.	The door **was slammed** by the girl.
A verb is **active** when the **subject** of the sentence **performs the action**.	A verb is **passive** when the **subject** of the sentence has the **action done to it**.

Practice

A. Underline verbs in these sentences and say whether they are active (A) or passive (P).

1. The snooker player <u>hit</u> the ball with his cue. (**A**)
2. The people were rescued by the helicopter. (__)
3. The treasure was buried by the pirates. (__)
4. The flash of lightning illuminated the night sky. (__)
5. The car was driven by a young man. (__)
6. The monkey jumped from the tree. (__)
7. Some foxes lived in the nearby wood. (__)
8. The teacher read a story to the class. (__)
9. The field was ploughed by the farmer. (__)
10. The pilot landed the aeroplane safely on the runway. (__)
11. The wedding dress was worn by the young bride. (__)
12. I spent a lot of money on sweets. (__)

Extension

B. Complete the passive verb in each sentence in a suitable way.

1. The car was _____ too fast by the foolish motorist.

2. The ball was _____ hard by the tennis player.

3. The cup was _____ convincingly by the school team.

4. The precious jewels were _____ by a thief.

5. The cake was _____ by Amy.

6. The telephone was _____ by the butler.

7. Many books were _____ by Roald Dahl.

8. A new song was _____ by the pop singer.

9. The baggy trousers were _____ by the funny clown.

10. The diver was _____ by a man-eating shark.

Challenge

C. Underline the passive verbs in these sentences.

Rewrite each sentence and change the verb from the passive to the active form.

1. The cases were carried by the porter. _____

2. Some seeds were planted by the man. _____

3. The tall beanstalk was grown by Jack. _____

4. Guitars are played by some pop stars. _____

5. The meal was served by the waiter. _____

6. The car was driven by Dr Hill. _____

7. Mountains are climbed by mountaineers. _____

8. A mouse was caught by the owl. _____

9. Some bread rolls were made by the baker. _____

10. Tom was looked after by the nurse. _____

TOPIC 17: **Vowels**

Focus

win	wine

watch

handl**e**	pizz**a**

Sometimes a **vowel** may have a **short** sound. Sometimes the same vowel may have a **long** sound.

Sometimes vowels **don't sound how we expect them to**!

The most **common** vowel at the **end of a word** is **e**. Other **vowels** are **less common**.

Practice

A. Add an e **to the end of each word. Write the new word you make.**

Say both words. Notice how the addition of the magic e **changes the sound of the vowel in the middle of the word.**

1. fat _____**fate**_____
2. mop _____
3. cub _____
4. dam _____
5. plum _____
6. can _____
7. hat _____
8. hid _____
9. kit _____
10. din _____
11. us _____
12. shin _____
13. slim _____
14. cut _____
15. strip _____
16. rob _____
17. not _____
18. cod _____
19. tub _____
20. hop _____
21. win _____

Extension

B. Make these words. In them the o sounds like ʊ!

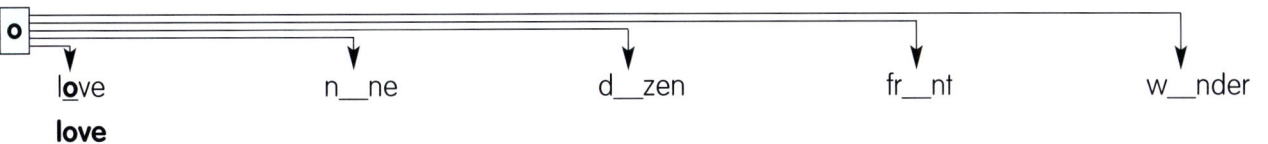

lo̲ve	n__ne	d__zen	fr__nt	w__nder
love				

C. Make these words. In them the a sounds like o!

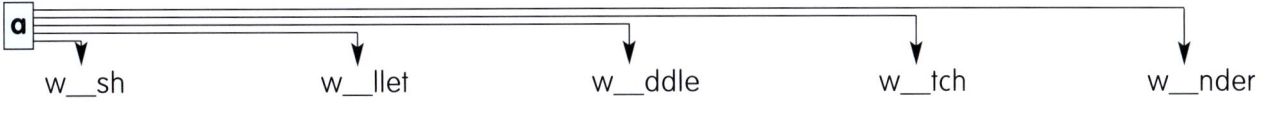

w__sh	w__llet	w__ddle	w__tch	w__nder

D. Make these words. In them the i sounds like a long e!

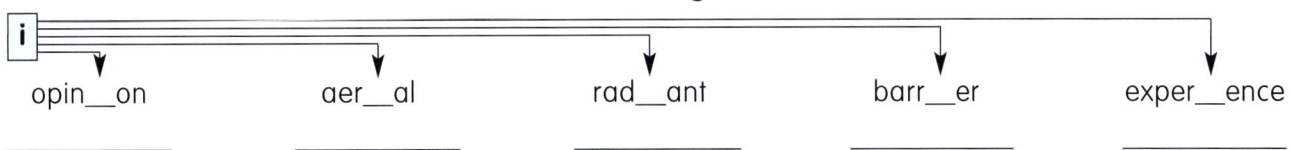

opin__on	aer__al	rad__ant	barr__er	exper__ence

Challenge

E. The nouns in the word box end with a vowel other than e. To make the plural of most nouns ending with the vowels a, i, o or u, we just add s e.g. ski – skis.

armadillo	banana	banjo	bongo	camera	cello	chapatti	cuckoo	dingo	emu
fiesta	gecko	igloo	kangaroo	kiwi	kimono	matzo	pasta	piano	piccolo
pizza	radio	risotto	samba	samosa	sauna	ski	sofa	tarantula	yoyo

Write the plural of each noun in the chart. Use a dictionary if necessary.

animal words	food words	music words	other words

TOPIC 18: **Standard English**

Focus

Standard English is the kind of language you are expected to use in school.

| Me and Sam was soaking. | | Sam and I were soaking. | |

Practice

A. Choose the correct form of the verb to complete each sentence.

1. The bees _____ (was/were) buzzing round the flowers.

2. What _____ (were/was) you doing last night?

3. We _____ (was/were) late for school.

4. Once upon a time there _____ (was/were) an ugly troll.

5. Tom _____ (bringed/brought) his new bike to my house.

6. I _____ (did/done) my homework quickly so I could go out.

7. They _____ (has/have) some good teachers at our school.

8. My mum _____ (give/gave) me a job to earn some money.

9. I _____ (see/saw) a very boring film at the weekend.

10. My friend _____ (don't/doesn't) like me any more.

11. I _____ (wish/wishes) I could go to Spain on holiday.

12. Sam _____ (run/ran) fast when the bull chased him.

B. Rewrite each sentence in Standard English. Avoid the use of double negatives.

1. There isn't no point in trying. _____

2. I don't want no sprouts. _____

3. I wasn't nowhere near him. _____

4. I don't read no books. _____

5. The girl didn't do nothing. _____

6. I never did nothing wrong. _____

7. The man never knew nobody. _____

8. I haven't won no prizes. _____

9. The boy hasn't been nowhere. _____

10. I didn't eat nothing nice. _____

Challenge

C. Rewrite each sentence in Standard English.

1. Last week me and Tom watches telly. _____

2. Who's got me comic? _____

3. They'se goin' out soon. _____

4. I could of done it easy. _____

5. I ain't eatin' nothing. _____

6. What you starin' at? _____

7. We was just leaving. _____

8. Here's the magazine what I bought. _____

9. We done it yesterday. _____

10. That's real nice of you. _____

TEST 3 (Score 1 mark for every correct answer.)

Topic 13

The four words below came into our language from French.

Match up each word with its meaning.

1. silhouette   someone paid to drive a car

2. souvenir   like a dark shadow

3. chauffeur   a counter where you can get refreshments

4. buffet   a keepsake

Topic 14

Rewrite each sentence. Begin the sentence with the adverb.

5. The old car rattled slowly along.   _____

6. The door suddenly opened.   _____

7. The children came in noisily.   _____

8. The old woman sat down wearily.   _____

Topic 15

Choose ie or ei to complete each word.

9. sh___ld   10. rec___ve

11. c___ling   12. bel___ve

Topic 16

Say whether the verb in each sentence is active (A) or passive (P).

13. The grass was cut by Mr Barton. (___)

14. Mrs Hill made a cup of coffee. (___)

15. The helicopter was flown by a young pilot. (___)

16. I caught a bad cold last week. (___)

Topic 17

Choose a, i or o to complete each word.

17. w___llet

18. fr___nt

19. opin___on

20. sw___rm

Topic 18

Write each sentence correctly in Standard English.

21. They was playing football. _____

22. He don't like me. _____

23. I never did nothing wrong. _____

24. Me and Ben went out. _____

Mark the test. Remember to fill in your score on page 3.

Write your score out of 24. ☐

Add a BONUS POINT if you scored 20 or more.

TOTAL SCORE FOR TEST 3 ☐

How did you find the test?

Colour a face

too hard   too easy   about right

TOPIC 19: **Some tricky spellings**

Focus

Always be on the lookout for tricky spellings!

For example, did you know that when **ar** comes after **w** it is often pronounced **or**, but when **or** comes after **w** it is often pronounced **er**?

says
ar = or
or = er

ar
or

a w**ar**m w**or**m

Practice

A. Complete each word with ar **or** or**.**

w**or**m	w**ar**m	w**or**ld	rew**ar**d	sw**ar**m
w**o**se	w**o**k	dw**ar**ves	w**o**rant	w**or**th

B. Use the words you made to complete each sentence.

1. Snow White met seven _dwarves_.

2. A _worm_ lives underground.

3. It is important always to _work_ hard.

4. The _world_ on which we live is part of a galaxy.

5. I like _warm_ weather better than the cold.

6. Two fifties are _worth_ a hundred.

7. A _swarm_ of angry wasps chased me.

8. My writing is getting _worse_ rather than better!

9. The police issued a _warrant_ for the thief's arrest.

10. Sam got a _reward_ for helping to catch the thief.

Extension

c ch sh

C. Complete each word with ch.

ch ips	ch emist	ma ch ine	ch orus	ch ocolate	ch ef	a ch e
para ch ute	ch estnut	ch ampagne	ch ase	stoma ch	bro ch ure	ben ch
ch auffeur	ch aracter	laun ch	s ch edule	ch oir	e ch o	

D. Write each word in the chart.

ch (sounds like "ach oo")	ch (sounds like **ck**)	ch (sounds like **sh**)
chips	chemist	machine

Challenge

E. Complete these words with cial, cious or cian.

1. musi**cian**
   <u>musician</u>

2. offi____
   _____

3. gra____
   _____

4. deli____
   _____

5. politi____
   _____

6. suspi_____
   _____

7. spe____
   _____

8. electri_____
   _____

9. so_____
   _____

F. What do you notice about the sound of ci in the words in part E?

G. Complete these words with tial or tious.

1. essen____
   _____

2. infec____
   _____

3. confiden____
   _____

4. ambi____
   _____

5. cau_____
   _____

6. ini____
   _____

H. What do you notice about the sound of ti in the words in part G?

TOPIC 20: **Clauses**

A **clause** is a **group of words** which may be used as a **whole sentence**, or as **part of a sentence**. A clause must contain a **subject** and a **verb**.

(subject) (verb)
↓ ↓

The ugly troll lived in a dark cave. | This is a **one-clause** sentence.

Practice

A. Underline the subject and circle the verb in each of these one-clause sentences.

1. The gardener mowed the grass.

2. Most wolves hunt in packs.

3. Some sheep were grazing in the field.

4. A green alien emerged from the spacecraft.

5. Dan drank a large bottle of fizzy lemonade.

6. Whales swim under the water most of the time.

7. Pandas eat bamboo shoots as their staple diet.

8. We found an old suit of armour in the castle.

9. Owls have good eyesight.

10. The naughty toddler stamped his foot angrily.

11. Some birds migrate to warmer countries in winter.

12. The fearsome-looking giant grabbed Jack by the arm.

Extension

B. Choose the best subject from the box to complete each one-clause sentence.

Underline the verb in each sentence to make sure there is only one!

The tree	We	A ship	The referee	Tailors
The ice	The wizard	Ben Nevis	Birds	The optician

1. _____ blew the whistle.

2. _____ cast a magic spell.

3. _____ eat worms.

4. _____ made the road slippery.

5. _____ is a Scottish mountain.

6. _____ make clothes.

7. _____ hit the reef in the storm.

8. _____ lost its leaves in winter.

9. _____ get wool from sheep.

10. _____ tested my eyes.

Challenge

C. Think of a suitable verb to complete each one-clause sentence.

Underline the subject in each sentence.

1. Foxes _____ in the woods.

2. The farmer _____ his field.

3. The stars _____ brightly at night.

4. Some birds _____ nests in trees.

5. Many cars _____ unleaded petrol.

6. An aeroplane _____ on the runway.

7. Thousands _____ the big match.

8. French people _____ on the right.

9. Tarantulas _____ huge and hairy.

10. Tortoises _____ in winter.

11. Trains _____ on rail lines.

12. A ferry _____ across the Channel.

13. Sam _____ the window.

14. Athletes _____ races.

15. Every snail _____ a shell.

16. Caterpillars _____ into butterflies.

17. I _____ a letter to my aunt.

18. The flag _____ on the flagpole.

19. Bees _____ honey.

20. The telephone _____ shrilly.

TOPIC 21: **Mnemonics**

A **mnemonic** is a **memory aid**.
We can use mnemonics to help us remember **tricky spellings**.

An island **is land** surrounded by water.

Practice

A. Underline the small word "hiding" inside each longer word in the word wall.

	believe	great	separate	
young	bicycle	piece	busy	
friend	ambitious	balloon	

B. Choose a word from above to complete each mnemonic.

1. The **bus** was _____.	**2.** Never _____ a **lie**.
3. I would like a _____ of **pie**.	**4.** A _____ looks like a **ball**.
5. _____ has a **rat** in it.	**6.** **You** are only _____ once.
7. I will be your _____ till the very **end**.	**8.** It's _____ to **eat**.
9. I am not a **bit** _____.	**10.** Don't ride a _____ in **icy** weather.

Extension

C. Choose a word from the box to complete each mnemonic.

fav**our**ite	w**eight**	**miser**able	con**science**	re**cog**nise
secretary	import**ant**	**govern**ment	**bread**th	ce**met**ery

1. What's the _____ of **eight** people?	2. A **miser** is always _____.
3. There's a **cog** in _____.	4. The chief **ant** is the most _____.
5. _____ is **our** best word.	6. _____ has **science** in it.
7. Three **e**'s are buried in a _____.	8. **Bread** has _____.
9. My _____ can keep a **secret**.	10. The _____ must **govern**.

Challenge

D. Make up some mnemonics of your own. Underline a small word inside each longer word.

Use it in your own mnemonic to help you remember the longer word.

vegetable	
chocolate	
skeleton	
cupboard	
headache	
sword	
temperature	
juice	
mathematics	
parallel	
soldier	
weather	
marriage	

TOPIC 22: **Compound sentences**

Focus

> **Remember** – A **clause** is a **group of words** which may be used as a **whole sentence**, or as **part of a sentence**. Every clause must contain a **subject** and a **verb**.

(subject)   (verb)

The squirrel climbed the tree.

This is a **one-clause** sentence.

> A **compound sentence** is made of **more than one clause**.

I picked the litter up   because it looked ugly.

(clause 1)   (clause 2)

Practice

A. Underline the verbs in these sentences. Say if each sentence consists of one or two clauses.

1. The cork floated on the surface of the water.   (**one**)
2. The dragon emerged from the cave.   (_____)
3. The clouds parted and the sun shone through.   (_____)
4. I ate my curry and rice hungrily.   (_____)
5. The race began after a while.   (_____)
6. Cats purr but dogs bark.   (_____)
7. I ran to the shop before it closed.   (_____)
8. The boy with the broken glasses answered correctly.   (_____)
9. Tom tackled two boys before he scored the goal.   (_____)
10. I hate weekends because they are so boring!   (_____)
11. The crowd clapped when the singer came on stage.   (_____)
12. My uncle who lives in America visited England last week.   (_____)

Extension

B. Match up the beginnings and endings of these compound sentences. Underline the verb in each clause.

The children <u>ran</u> fast	if you come with me.
This is the rose bush	how you can do it.
Mark sharpened his pencil	had a puncture.
The car that crashed	before he drew the picture.
I will go	because they <u>were</u> late.
The boy hurt himself	because I wanted some sweets.
I went to the shop	when he bumped his head.
I will tell you	that I planted.

Challenge

C. Rewrite each of these compound sentences as two separate sentences containing one clause.
(You may have to alter the wording slightly in some cases.) Circle the verbs in the sentences you write.

1. Anna picked some flowers and gave them to her mum.
    Anna picked some flowers. She gave them to her mum.

2. Tom is very tired because he ran a marathon race yesterday.
    _____

3. It poured with rain so we got soaking wet.
    _____

4. We went to the station and we caught the train.
    _____

5. I got all my spellings right but Emma did badly in the test.
    _____

6. I like swimming but I can't dive very well.
    _____

7. The greedy boy bought some sweets and ate them all himself.
    _____

8. We started early and arrived at the hotel by lunchtime.
    _____

9. The woman bought some wool and knitted a jumper for her husband.
    _____

10. I tried to do my homework but it was too difficult for me.
    _____

TOPIC 23: **Connectives**

Focus

Connectives are **words or phrases** that can **join** together **ideas** or **sentences**.

The burglar broke the window **so that** he could get in.

Sometimes a connective may come **at the beginning** of the sentence.

Unless you tidy your room,
you won't get any pocket money.

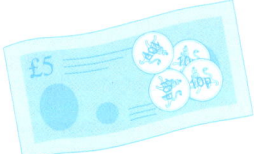

Practice

A. Choose the best connective to join the pairs of clauses together.

1. It was very cold _____ (since/so) it was a relief to reach home.

2. It is hard to learn the violin _____ (if/unless) you are prepared to practise.

3. I saved up _____ (so that/as) I could buy a TV.

4. I always try to do my homework _____ (although/before) I watch TV.

5. I like to wear my wellingtons _____ (and/whenever) it rains a lot.

6. The baby didn't stop crying _____ (until/during) she had a drink.

7. My toy has been broken _____ (since/when) I accidentally trod on it.

8. I listened to the music _____ (although/while) it was terrible.

9. I got out the mower _____ (if/because) the grass needed cutting.

10. I cleaned my teeth _____ (while/before) I went to bed.

11. I stayed awake _____ (so/as long as) I was able to.

12. I like coffee _____ (whereas/because) I hate tea.

Extension

B. Underline the connectives in these sentences. Rewrite each sentence, beginning with the connective.

1. I enjoyed the party **even though** I didn't think I would.

   Even though I didn't think I would, I enjoyed the party.

2. Mrs Barnes hung out the washing after the washing machine had finished.

   _____

3. Mr Green hummed to himself while he was having a bath.

   _____

4. I will always be your friend as long as you want me to.

   _____

5. I love to visit museums whenever I have time.

   _____

6. You can't have any pudding because you didn't eat your cabbage.

   _____

7. Do you go swimming whenever you can?

   _____

8. We will buy some doughnuts if we have enough money.

   _____

Challenge

C. Make up some two-clause sentences of your own. Use these connectives to join the clauses.

because	although
wherever	until
whereas	in order to
as long as	unless
so that	nevertheless

_____

_____

_____

_____

_____

_____

_____

_____

_____

TOPIC 24: **Playing about with words**

Focus

Playing with words can help us **learn** more **about spelling**.

nips – spin

noon

care – race

Semordnilaps are words that may be spelt **backwards** to make another word.

Palindromes are words which are spelt the **same backwards** or **forwards**.

An **anagram** mixes up the letters of a word to make another word.

Practice

A. Write each of these words backwards to make another word.

1. star ___**rats**___
2. evil _____
3. keep _____
4. moor _____
5. gulp _____
6. part _____
7. spot _____
8. pans _____
9. paws _____
10. bats _____
11. step _____
12. reed _____
13. pots _____
14. now _____
15. emit _____
16. flog _____

B. Tick ✔ which of these words are semordnilaps.

1. dew ☐
2. taste ☐
3. dark ☐
4. gas ☐
5. liar ☐
6. moon ☐
7. loop ☐
8. into ☐
9. pine ☐
10. net ☐
11. flow ☐
12. paper ☐
13. pens ☐
14. devil ☐
15. brag ☐
16. hand ☐
17. was ☐
18. foot ☐
19. tub ☐
20. fuel ☐

Extension

C. Say whether each word is a semordnilap (S) or a palindrome (P).

1. civic (_____)   2. are (_____)   3. mum (_____)   4. level (_____)

5. mug (_____)   6. net (_____)   7. solos (_____)   8. doom (_____)

9. radar (_____)   10. nap (_____)   11. noon (_____)   12. madam (_____)

13. moor (_____)   14. eye (_____)   15. evil (_____)   16. deed (_____)

17. reed (_____)   18. peep (_____)   19. eve (_____)   20. rotor (_____)

Challenge

D. Work out the following anagrams.

word	anagram
mace	came
aids	
ales	
art	
rife	
cafe	
deal	
lamp	
scare	
bore	
clean	
design	
plane	
stare	

word	anagram
miles	
asleep	
stale	
earth	
risen	
snap	
warder	
peach	
drop	
state	
wasp	
priest	
prides	
oils	

TEST 4

Topic 19

Complete each word with ar **or** or.

1. w___ld

2. w___th

3. w___der

4. w___ts

Topic 20

Underline the subject and circle the verb in each one-clause sentence.

5. The boy climbed the tree.

6. My cat likes cream.

7. Carpenters make things from wood.

8. Mr Douglas closed the door.

Topic 21

Find and underline a small word "hiding" inside each of these tricky words.

9. friend

10. piece

11. great

12. young

Topic 22

Say whether each sentence contains one or two clauses.

13. I switched on the light. (_____)

14. I undressed before I got into bed. (_____)

15. I like sprouts but I hate cabbage! (_____)

16. The crowd cheered wildly. (_____)

Topic 23

Choose the best connective to complete each sentence.

17. It was hot _____ (since/so) I took off my coat.

18. You can't have a cake _____ (if/unless) you buy it yourself.

19. We didn't reach home _____ (until/during) it was midnight.

20. I finished my book _____ (while/before) I turned out the light.

Topic 24

(Questions 21–24) Match up the anagrams in Set A and Set B.

Set A	deal	warder	slate	blame
Set B	reward	amble	lead	steal

Mark the test. Now add up all your test scores and put your final score on page 3.

Write your score out of 24. [_____]

Add a BONUS POINT if you scored 20 or more.

TOTAL SCORE FOR TEST 4 [_____]

How did you find the test?

Colour a face

too hard   too easy   about right

Answers

TOPIC 1: **Common letter strings** (page 4)

A.

1. illust**rate**; edu**cate**; choco**late**; sepa**rate**; delibe**rate**; conside**rate**
2. ath**lete**; com**plete**; com**plete**; de**lete**; con**crete**; obso**lete**
3. defi**nite**; favou**rite**; dyna**mite**; oppo**site**; po**lite**; re**cite**

B.

frag<u>rant</u>/arro<u>gant</u>
ba<u>dge</u>/he<u>dge</u>hog
<u>crouch</u>/<u>touch</u>
fac<u>tory</u>/s<u>tory</u>
dist<u>urb</u>/b<u>urg</u>le
<u>fruit</u>/b<u>ruise</u>
pla<u>que</u>/anti<u>que</u>
be<u>aten</u>/sw<u>eaty</u>
ton<u>gue</u>/catalo<u>gue</u>
ware<u>house</u>/sc<u>ared</u>

C.

The correct letter strings are underlined. The words used are examples only (other answers are possible).
Left-hand column: sec<u>tor</u>; ad<u>venture</u>; <u>slice</u>; gene<u>rous</u>; <u>taught</u>; vegeta<u>rian</u>; sh<u>eer</u>
Right-hand column: mili<u>tary</u>; <u>trough</u>; carni<u>val</u>; un<u>less</u>; tole<u>rance</u>; fa<u>vourite</u>; pinn<u>acle</u>

TOPIC 2: **Parts of speech – nouns** (page 6)

A.

names of people	names of places	names of things
doctor	dock	orange
astronaut	hangar	moon
dentist	bank	lorry
carpenter	library	cup
plumber	church	pencil
editor	stadium	computer
	factory	leaf

B.

1. <u>Mount Kilimanjaro</u> is the highest mountain in <u>Africa</u>.
2. <u>Edinburgh</u> is the capital city of <u>Scotland</u>.
3. I bought a copy of the <u>Daily Mirror</u> and the <u>TV Times</u>.
4. Yesterday was <u>Thursday</u>, the first day of <u>December</u>.
5. <u>Sir Francis Drake</u> was a sailor in the reign of <u>Queen Elizabeth the First</u>.
6. We went to the <u>Gaumont Cinema</u> in <u>Luton</u>.

C.

1. strength   2. courage   3. poverty   4. fear   5. speed   6. belief

D.

Personal answers.

TOPIC 3: **Double letters** (page 8)

A.

root word	+ suffix **er**	+ suffix **est**	+ suffix **ing**	+ suffix **ed**
hop	hopper	—	hopping	hopped
skip	skipper	—	skipping	skipped
bat	batter	—	batting	batted
hum	hummer	—	humming	hummed
sad	sadder	saddest	—	—
fit	fitter	fittest	fitting	fitted
plan	planner	—	planning	planned
jog	jogger	—	jogging	jogged
hot	hotter	hottest	—	—
flat	flatter	flattest	—	—
big	bigger	biggest	—	—
ban	banner	—	banning	banned
but	butter	—	butting	butted
wet	wetter	wettest	wetting	wetted

B.

1. terror   2. arrive   3. banner   4. barrow   5. dinner
6. ribbon   7. lesson   8. message   9. flurry   10. carry
11. common   12. marriage   13. summer   14. rummage   15. rabbit
16. borrow   17. hammer   18. burrow   19. carriage   20. horror

C.

1. ter/ror   2. ar/rive   3. ban/ner   4. bar/row   5. din/ner
6. rib/bon   7. les/son   8. mes/sage   9. flur/ry   10. car/ry
11. com/mon   12. mar/riage   13. sum/mer   14. rum/mage   15. rab/bit
16. bor/row   17. ham/mer   18. bur/row   19. car/riage   20. hor/ror

D.

1. ✓   2. ✗ omitting   3. ✗ marvellous   4. ✓
5. ✓   6. ✗ deterrent   7. ✗ rebellion   8. ✓
9. ✓   10. ✗ traveller   11. ✓   12. ✗ forgotten
13. ✗ permitting   14. ✓   15. ✗ metallic   16. ✓
17. ✓   18. ✗ incurring   19. ✓   20. ✗ levelled

TOPIC 4: **Parts of speech – verbs** (page 10)

A.

1. Pr   2. P   3. F   4. Pr   5. P   6. F   7. Pr   8. P   9. F   10. Pr   11. P
12. F   13. Pr   14. P   15. F   16. Pr   17. P   18. F   19. Pr   20. P   21. F   22. P

B.

1. is/Pr   2. was/P   3. am/Pr   4. were/P   5. will/F   6. have/P
7. has/P   8. will/F   9. is/Pr   10. was/P   11. is/Pr   12. was/P
13. am/Pr   14. were/P   15. will/F   16. have/P

C.

1. If you are tired you ^ should go to bed.
2. I ^ would buy the video game if I had enough money.
3. I ^ could cross the road if it wasn't so busy.
4. I told you that if you practised you ^ would get better.
5. If horses had wings they ^ could fly!
6. You ^ should not stay out in direct sunshine too long.
7. I ^ could or would not eat my dinner because it was cold.
8. I ^ would be grateful if you help me.
9. If I buy a ticket I ^ might win.
10. ^ Might I play with your toy if I promise not to break it?

TOPIC 5: **Prefixes** (page 12)

A.

1. automobile   2. bilingual   3. disagree   4. extraordinary
5. illegal   6. interview   7. microscope   8. aquaplane
9. submarine   10. superhuman   11. prehistoric   12. centimetre
13. disappear   14. bicycle   15. surplus   16. inland
17. semicircle   18. outdo   19. unwell   20. export

B.

prefix	meaning of prefix	word	definition
in	opposite of	**in**secure	not secure
tri	three	**tri**angle	a three-sided shape
semi	half	**semi**circle	half a circle
non	not	**non**sense	something that doesn't make sense
post	after, behind	**post**script	a message added to a letter as an afterthought
mis	bad, wrong	**mis**behave	behave badly
re	again	**re**play	play again
peri	around	**peri**meter	the distance around something
under	beneath	**under**current	current beneath the surface
with	back	**with**draw	draw back
equi	equal	**equi**lateral	equal-sided

C.

The words in the table below are examples only. Many answers are possible.

prefix	two words beginning with the prefix		meaning of prefix
anti	antiseptic	antibiotic	against
aero	aeroplane	aerodrome	air
geo	geography	geology	earth
tele	television	telescope	from afar
super	superstar	supernatural	over, beyond
mono	monopoly	monotonous	alone, single
auto	automatic	automobile	independently
multi	multiply	multiplex	many
mini	minimal	minimum	small
uni	universal	unify	one
inter	interrupt	interactive	between, among
ex	export	exchange	out of
fore	foreboding	forearm	in front of

TOPIC 6: **Parts of speech – adjectives** (page 14)

A.

1. sunny/hot
2. huge/thrilling
3. hungry/tired/thirsty
4. old/little/thatched
5. ancient/bony
6. magnificent/beautiful
7. first/brilliant/red
8. shaggy/black/juicy
9. rough/woollen
10. weary/disheartened
11. strange/metallic
12. foreign/little

B.

adjectives to do with:			
colour	size	feelings	taste
red	huge	scared	sweet
brown	thin	amazed	salty
yellow	short	bored	spicy
silver	tall	happy	sour

C and **D.**
Personal answers.

TEST 1 (page 16)

Topic 1 1. tory 2. que 3. ar 4. ice

Topic 2 5. kno**w**led**g**e 6. e**x**pe**c**tation 7. su**cc**ess 8. thou**g**ht

Topic 3 9. battle 10. rubbish 11. terror 12. tennis

Topic 4 13. F 14. P 15. Pr 16. F

Topic 5 17. surface 18. subway 19. semicircle 20. supermarket

Topic 6 Other answers are possible.

21. full 22. wide 23. wild 24. sharp

TOPIC 7: **Synonyms** (page 18)

A.

The third synonyms (in brackets below) are examples only.
begin/start/(commence)
wide/broad/(expanded)
strike/hit/(beat)
go/leave/(depart)
hurry/rush/(dash)

narrow/thin/(confined)
clever/intelligent/(smart)
nasty/horrible/(unpleasant)
call/shout/(yell)
hard/difficult/(demanding)

B.

The third synonyms (in brackets below) are examples only.
1. right/(accurate)
2. misfortune/(disaster)
3. scorn/(dislike)
4. horrible/(ugly)
5. calm/(peaceful)
6. separate/(break)
7. edge/(limit)
8. damp/(wet)
9. stubborn/(firm)
10. pause/(dither)
11. surprise/(amaze)
12. fret/(agonise)

C.
Personal answers.

TOPIC 8: **Parts of speech – adverbs** (page 20)

A.

Examples only (many answers are possible):
1. quickly
2. fashionably
3. suddenly
4. happily
5. loudly
6. merrily
7. carefully
8. unhappily
9. quietly
10. heavily
11. patiently
12. brilliantly

B.

1. quietly
2. usually
3. happily
4. awkwardly
5. angrily
6. fairly
7. sadly
8. equally
9. pleasantly
10. cleverly

C.

For example:
1. I sighed unhappily.
2. The children spoke quietly.
3. I put my clothes untidily on the chair.
4. I did all my sums correctly.
5. The nurse treated me harshly.
6. The river flowed slowly.
7. The boy spoke rudely.
8. I did my writing carefully.
9. The thief answered dishonestly.
10. The child spoke unclearly.

TOPIC 9: **Common sayings** (page 22)

A.

The early bird catches the worm. New brooms sweep clean. A fool and his money are soon parted. No news is good news. Practice makes perfect. Great minds think alike. Still waters run deep. A friend in need is a friend indeed. One good turn deserves another. Early to bed early to rise. A bad workman blames his tools. An apple a day keeps the doctor away.

B.

to put the cart before the horse – to do things the wrong way round; to sit on the fence – to refuse to take sides in an argument; to hang your head – to be ashamed of yourself; to strike while the iron is hot – to act while conditions are favourable; to face the music – to take punishment without complaint; to hit below the belt – to act unfairly; to hit the nail on the head – to be exactly right; to kick up a dust – to create a row; to hold one's tongue – to keep silent; to burn the candle at both ends – to overdo work and play

C.

Suggested answers:
1. Leave your options open.
2. A person who keeps moving doesn't collect much or achieve much.
3. What one person loves another person will hate.
4. Do what you can while the conditions are good.
5. People who know the least, speak the most.
6. Don't overstretch yourself.
7. People associate with people who are similar to them.
8. There is something good in every bad situation.
9. From one problem to a worse problem.
10. Don't assume anything before it has happened.

TOPIC 10: **Parts of speech – pronouns** (page 24)

A.
1. Sophie/the cat
2. the trainers/Tom
3. the twins
4. Ben/the baby
5. their friends
6. Jenny

B.
1. mine
2. his
3. your
4. yours
5. its
6. theirs

C.
1. 1st person singular
2. 3rd person singular
3. 3rd person plural
4. 3rd person singular
5. 3rd person singular
6. 1st person plural
7. 2nd person singular
8. 2nd person plural

D.
1. it
2. you
3. I
4. they
5. She
6. He

E.

Sam did not like the woods at night. <u>He</u> could hear strange sounds all around. <u>He</u> decided to get out of there as quickly as possible. <u>He</u> began to run. Just then Sam heard an even louder noise. <u>He</u> stopped. <u>He</u> peered into the darkness but <u>he</u> could see nothing. Soon Sam was out of the woods. <u>He</u> was safe at last!

F.

I did not like the woods at night. I could hear strange sounds all around. I decided to get out of there as quickly as possible. I began to run. Just then I heard an even louder noise. I stopped. I peered into the darkness but I could see nothing. Soon I was out of the woods. I was safe at last!

TOPIC 11: **Suffixes** (page 26)

A.

Set 1: dangerous; perilous; mountainous; poisonous
Set 2: famous; nervous; adventurous; ridiculous
Set 3: mysterious; furious; luxurious; glorious

B.

Set 1: The spelling of the noun remained the **same** when **ous** was added.
Set 2: In this set of words, the letter **e** at the end of the words was **removed** before the suffix **ous** was added.
Set 3: In the words in this set, the letter **y** was changed to **i** before the suffix **ous** was added.

C.

adjective	noun
beautiful	beauty
hungry	hunger
responsible	response
wondrous	wonder
argumentative	argument
glorious	glory
circular	circle
fortunate	fortune

adjective	noun
roguish	rogue
awful	awe
Portuguese	Portugal
gigantic	giant
memorable	memory
metallic	metal
furry	fur
natural	nature

D.

noun	adjective
nation	national
adventure	adventurous
water	watery
athlete	athletic
force	forceful
secret	secretive
tragedy	tragic
victory	victorious

noun	adjective
smoke	smoky
plenty	plentiful
centre	central
Canada	Canadian
response	responsive
fame	famous
poet	poetic
Brazil	Brazilian

TOPIC 12: **Parts of speech – prepositions** (page 28)

A.

four letters:	down	from	near	over	upon
five letters:	above	below	under
six letters:	across	behind
seven letters:	between	through

B.

1. **a**bove 2. **a**cross 3. **b**ehind 4. **b**elow 5. **b**etween 6. **d**own
7. **f**rom 8. **n**ear 9. **o**ver 10. **t**hrough 11. **u**nder 12. **u**pon

C.

on/off; above/below; over/under; down/up; inside/outside; with/without; from/to; after/before

D.

1. th**u**nder 2. s**u**pplier 3. r**a**inbow 4. **o**ffice
5. h**o**vered 6. p**o**nd 7. D**o**ver 8. r**a**fters

E.

For example (other answers may be possible):
1. to 2. with 3. for 4. to 5. with 6. for 7. into
8. of 9. for 10. about 11. of 12. with 13. of 14. of
15. with 16. for 17. about 18. for 19. with 20. to 21. of

TEST 2 (page 30)

Topic 7	1–4. clever/intelligent; peaceful/calm; strike/hit; commence/start

Topic 8	5. gently/roughly	6. rapidly/slowly	7. politely/rudely	8. merrily/sadly
Topic 9	9. vessels	10. minds	11. bird	12. broom
Topic 10	13. Ben	14. the wind	15. the twins	16. Emma and Amy
Topic 11	17. beautiful	18. adventurous	19. responsible	20. fortunate
Topic 12	21. above	22. outside	23. over	24. beneath

TOPIC 13: **Word origins** (page 32)

A.

et sounds like **ay** in **day**	et sounds like **et** in **wet**
duvet	trumpet
sachet	banquet
ballet	scarlet
bouquet	bracket
cabaret	blanket

B.

1. duvet 2. Scarlet 3. bouquet 4. Ballet 5. sachet
6. bracket 7. trumpet 8. banquet 9. blanket 10. cabaret

C.

words from Italian	words from Spanish
piano	tomato
ballerina	banana
opera	potato
soprano	galleon
violin	chocolate
concert	hurricane

D.

pyjamas – shirt and trousers to sleep in; verandah – an open porch; shampoo – something that cleans hair; bungalow – a house with only one storey

E.

Greek root word	meaning	English word
aster	star	astrology
bios	life	biology
kosmos	beauty	cosmetic
logos	word/speech	dialogue
metron	a measure	metre
pathos	suffering	pathetic
phone	sound	microphone
polis	city	politics
gramma	letter/thing written	grammar
tele	from afar	television
sphaira	globe/ball	sphere
optikus	to do with sight	optician

TOPIC 14: **Word order** (page 34)

A.

1. The old car rattled noisily along the street. | Noisily the old car rattled along the street.
2. Anna quickly did her homework. | Quickly Anna did her homework.
3. The thief crept quietly around the house. | Quietly the thief crept around the house.
4. Sam dribbled past his opponent skilfully. | Skilfully Sam dribbled past his opponent.
5. The wind got up suddenly. | Suddenly the wind got up.
6. I did my best writing neatly in my book. | Neatly in my book I did my best writing.
7. Tom smiled at his old aunt sweetly. | Sweetly Tom smiled at his old aunt.
8. The carthorse plodded tiredly up the hill. | Tiredly the carthorse plodded up the hill.
9. I gasped breathlessly, "I can't go on!" | Breathlessly I gasped, "I can't go on!"
10. Tara accepted the winning cup graciously. | Graciously Tara accepted the winning cup.

B.

1. We will go out if the weather is fine. | If the weather is fine, we will go out.
2. Jack read a book while I ate my tea. | While I ate my tea, Jack read a book.
3. Mum is not happy unless we are good. | Unless we are good, Mum is not happy.
4. The crowd cheered as the band played. | As the band played, the crowd cheered.
5. We can go out when our uncle arrives. | When our uncle arrives, we can go out.
6. I would buy a car if I won a lot of money. | If I won a lot of money, I would buy a car.
7. The bell rang while I was in the bath. | While I was in the bath, the bell rang.
8. You can't see unless you open your eyes! | Unless you open your eyes, you can't see!
9. I limped badly as I walked along. | As I walked along, I limped badly.
10. A child was hurt when the car crashed. | When the car crashed, a child was hurt.

C.

1. We went on holiday to France.
2. When he stopped, Tom had a drink.
3. At night the owl hunted for prey.
4. Suddenly the car stopped.
5. Shyly the girl looked at the boy.
6. As she came in, the woman laughed.
7. Out of the woods the bear appeared.
8. Under the old oak tree sat a child.
9. Please shut the door.
10. In the bag there were six apples.

TOPIC 15: **Spelling rules** (page 36)

A.

1. thief; field; shield; piece; niece 2. brief; fierce; pierce; achieve; believe

B.

1. shriek 2. receive 3. priest 4. ceiling 5. mischief
6. piece 7. deceive 8. shield 9. relief 10. conceit
11. yield 12. believe 13. receipt 14. grief 15. perceive

C.

1. ✓ 2. ✗ noticeable 3. ✗ changeable 4. ✓
5. ✗ courageous 6. ✗ advantageous 7. ✓ 8. ✓
9. ✓ 10. ✗ enforceable 11. ✓ 12. ✗ outrageous

D.

Personal answers.

TOPIC 16: **Active and passive verbs** (page 38)

A.
1. The snooker player <u>hit</u> the ball with his cue. (A)
2. The people <u>were rescued</u> by the helicopter. (P)
3. The treasure <u>was buried</u> by the pirates. (P)
4. The flash of lightning <u>illuminated</u> the night sky. (A)
5. The car <u>was driven</u> by a young man. (P)
6. The monkey <u>jumped</u> from the tree. (A)
7. Some foxes <u>lived</u> in the nearby wood. (A)
8. The teacher <u>read</u> a story to the class. (A)
9. The field <u>was ploughed</u> by the farmer. (P)
10. The pilot <u>landed</u> the aeroplane safely on the runway. (A)
11. The wedding dress <u>was worn</u> by the young bride. (P)
12. I <u>spent</u> a lot of money on sweets. (A)

B.
For example (other answers may be possible):
1. driven 2. hit 3. won 4. stolen 5. baked
6. answered 7. written 8. recorded 9. worn 10. attacked

C.
1. The cases <u>were carried</u> by the porter. The porter carried the cases.
2. Some seeds <u>were planted</u> by the man. The man planted some seeds.
3. The tall beanstalk <u>was grown</u> by Jack. Jack grew the tall beanstalk.
4. Guitars <u>are played</u> by some pop stars. Some pop stars play guitars.
5. The meal <u>was served</u> by the waiter. The waiter served the meal.
6. The car <u>was driven</u> by Dr Hill. Dr Hill drove the car.
7. Mountains <u>are climbed</u> by mountaineers. Mountaineers climb mountains.
8. A mouse <u>was caught</u> by the owl. The owl caught a mouse.
9. Some bread rolls <u>were made</u> by the baker. The baker made some bread rolls.
10. Tom <u>was looked</u> after by the nurse. The nurse looked after Tom.

TOPIC 17: **Vowels** (page 40)

A.
1. fate 2. mope 3. cube 4. dame 5. plume 6. cane 7. hate
8. hide 9. kite 10. dine 11. use 12. shine 13. slime 14. cute
15. stripe 16. robe 17. note 18. code 19. tube 20. hope 21. wine

B.
love; none; dozen; front; wonder

C.
wash; wallet; waddle; watch; wander

D.
opinion; aerial; radiant; barrier; experience

E.

animal words	food words	music words	other words
armadillos	bananas	banjos	cameras
cuckoos	chapattis	bongos	igloos
dingoes	matzos	cellos	kimonos
emus	pastas	fiestas	saunas
geckos (**or** oes)	pizzas	pianos	skis
kangaroos	risottos	piccolos	sofas
kiwis	samosas	radios	yoyos
tarantulas		sambas	

TOPIC 18: **Standard English** (page 42)

A.
1. were 2. were 3. were 4. was 5. brought 6. did
7. have 8. gave 9. saw 10. doesn't 11. wish 12. ran

B.
1. There isn't any point in trying. 2. I don't want any sprouts.
3. I wasn't anywhere near him. 4. I don't read any books.
5. The girl didn't do anything. 6. I never did anything wrong.
7. The man didn't know anybody. 8. I haven't won any prizes.
9. The boy hasn't been anywhere. 10. I didn't eat anything nice.

C.
1. Last week Tom and I watched television. 2. Who's got my comic?
3. They're going out soon. 4. I could have done it easily.
5. I'm not eating anything. 6. What are you staring at?
7. We were just leaving. 8. Here's the magazine that I bought.
9. We did it yesterday. 10. That's really nice of you.

TEST 3 (page 44)

Topic 13	1. like a dark shadow		2. a keepsake

Topic 13 1. like a dark shadow 2. a keepsake
3. someone paid to drive a car 4. a counter where you can get refreshments
Topic 14 5. Slowly the old car rattled along. 6. Suddenly the door opened.
7. Noisily the children came in. 8. Wearily the old woman sat down.
Topic 15 9. shield 10. receive 11. ceiling 12. believe
Topic 16 13. P 14. A 15. P 16. A
Topic 17 17. wallet 18. front 19. opinion 20. swarm
Topic 18 21. They were playing football. 22. He doesn't like me.
23. I never did anything wrong. 24. Ben and I went out.

TOPIC 19: **Some tricky spellings** (page 46)

A.

w**or**m	w**ar**m	w**or**ld	rew**ar**d	sw**ar**m
w**or**se	w**or**k	dw**ar**ves	w**ar**rant	w**or**th

B.
1. dwarves 2. worm 3. work 4. world 5. warm
6. worth 7. swarm 8. worse 9. warrant 10. reward

C.

chips	**ch**emist	ma**ch**ine	**ch**orus	**ch**ocolate	**ch**ef	a**ch**e
para**ch**ute	**ch**estnut	**ch**ampagne	**ch**ase	stoma**ch**	bro**ch**ure	
ben**ch**	**ch**auffeur	**ch**aracter	laun**ch**	s**ch**edule	**ch**oir	e**ch**o

D.

ch (sounds like "a**ch**oo")	**ch** (sounds like **ck**)	**ch** (sounds like **sh**)
chips	chemist	machine
chocolate	chorus	chef
chestnut	ache	parachute
chase	stomach	champagne
bench	character	brochure
launch	choir	chauffeur
	echo	schedule

E.
1. musi**cian** 2. offi**cial** 3. gra**cious**
4. deli**cious** 5. politi**cian** 6. suspi**cious**
7. spe**cial** 8. electri**cian** 9. so**cial**

F.
In the words in question E, the **ci** sounds like **sh**.

G.
1. essen**tial** 2. infec**tious** 3. confiden**tial**
4. ambi**tious** 5. cau**tious** 6. ini**tial**

H.
In the words in question G, the **ti** sounds like **sh**.

TOPIC 20: **Clauses** (page 48)

A.
1. The gardener (mowed) the grass.
2. Most wolves (hunt) in packs.
3. Some sheep (were grazing) in the field.
4. A green alien (emerged) from the spacecraft.
5. Dan (drank) a large bottle of fizzy lemonade.
6. Whales (swim) under the water most of the time.
7. Pandas (eat) bamboo shoots as their staple diet.
8. We (found) an old suit of armour in the castle.
9. Owls (have) good eyesight.
10. The naughty toddler (stamped) his foot angrily.
11. Some birds (migrate) to warmer countries in winter.
12. The fearsome-looking giant (grabbed) Jack by the arm.

B.
1. The referee 2. The wizard 3. Birds 4. The ice 5. Ben Nevis
6. Tailors 7. A ship 8. The tree 9. We 10. The optician

C.

The words in brackets are examples only.

1. Foxes (live) in the woods.
2. The farmer (ploughed) his field.
3. The stars (shine) brightly at night.
4. Some birds (build) nests in trees.
5. Many cars (use) unleaded petrol.
6. An aeroplane (landed) on the runway.
7. Thousands (attended) the big match.
8. French people (drive) on the right.
9. Tarantulas (are) huge and hairy.
10. Tortoises (hibernate) in winter.
11. Trains (run) on rail lines.
12. A ferry (sailed) across the Channel.
13. Sam (opened) the window.
14. Athletes (run) races.
15. Every snail (has) a shell.
16. Caterpillars (turn) into butterflies.
17. I (sent) a letter to my aunt.
18. The flag (fluttered) on the flagpole.
19. Bees (make) honey.
20. The telephone (rang) shrilly.

TOPIC 21: **Mnemonics** (page 50)

A.

	bel**ie**ve	gr**ea**t	sep**a**r**a**te	
young	bic**y**cle	p**ie**ce	bu**s**y	
	fri**e**nd	amb**i**tious	ba**ll**oon	

B.

1. The **bus** was **busy**.
2. Never **believe** a **lie**.
3. I would like a **piece** of **pie**.
4. A **balloon** looks like a **ball**.
5. **Separate** has a **rat** in it.
6. **You** are only **young** once.
7. I will be your **friend** till the very **end**.
8. It's **great** to **eat**.
9. I am not a **bit ambitious**.
10. Don't ride a **bicycle** in **icy** weather.

C.

1. What's the w**eight** of **eight** people?
2. A **miser** is always **miser**able.
3. There's a **cog** in re**cog**nise.
4. The chief **ant** is the most import**ant**.
5. Fav**our**ite is **our** best word.
6. Con**science** has **science** in it.
7. Three **e**'s are buried in a c**e**m**e**t**e**ry.
8. **Bread** has **bread**th.
9. My **secret**ary can keep a **secret**.
10. The **govern**ment must **govern**.

D.

Personal answers.

TOPIC 22: **Compound sentences** (page 52)

A.

1. The cork floated on the surface of the water. (one)
2. The dragon emerged from the cave. (one)
3. The clouds parted and the sun shone through. (two)
4. I ate my curry and rice hungrily. (one)
5. The race began after a while. (one)
6. Cats purr but dogs bark. (two)
7. I ran to the shop before it closed. (two)
8. The boy with the broken glasses answered correctly. (one)
9. Tom tackled two boys before he scored the goal. (two)
10. I hate weekends because they are so boring! (two)
11. The crowd clapped when the singer came on stage. (two)
12. My uncle who lives in America visited England last week. (two)

B.

The children ran fast because they were late.
This is the rose bush that I planted.
Mark sharpened his pencil before he drew the picture.
The car that crashed had a puncture.
I will go if you come with me.
The boy hurt himself when he bumped his head.
I went to the shop because I wanted some sweets.
I will tell you how you can do it.

C.

1. Anna (picked) some flowers. She (gave) them to her mum.
2. Tom (is) very tired. He (ran) a marathon race yesterday.
3. It (poured) with rain. We (got) soaking wet.
4. We (went) to the station. We (caught) the train.
5. I (got) all my spellings right. Emma (did) badly in the test.
6. I like swimming. I (can't dive) very well.
7. The greedy boy (bought) some sweets. He (ate) them all himself.
8. We (started) early. We (arrived) at the hotel by lunchtime.
9. The woman (bought) some wool. She (knitted) a jumper for her husband.
10. I (tried) to do my homework. It (was) too difficult for me.

TOPIC 23: **Connectives** (page 54)

A.

1. so
2. unless
3. so that
4. before
5. whenever
6. until
7. since
8. although
9. because
10. before
11. as long as
12. whereas

B.

1. I enjoyed the party even though I didn't think I would.
   Even though I didn't think I would, I enjoyed the party.
2. Mrs Barnes hung out the washing after the washing machine had finished.
   After the washing machine had finished, Mrs Barnes hung out the washing.
3. Mr Green hummed to himself while he was having a bath.
   While he was having a bath, Mr Green hummed to himself.
4. I will always be your friend as long as you want me to.
   As long as you want me to, I will always be your friend.
5. I love to visit museums whenever I have time.
   Whenever I have time, I love to visit museums.
6. You can't have any pudding because you didn't eat your cabbage.
   Because you didn't eat your cabbage, you can't have any pudding.
7. Do you go swimming whenever you can?
   Whenever you can, do you go swimming?
8. We will buy some doughnuts if we have enough money.
   If we have enough money, we will buy some doughnuts.

C.

Personal answers.

TOPIC 24: **Playing about with words** (page 56)

A.

1. rats
2. live
3. peek
4. room
5. plug
6. trap
7. tops
8. snap
9. swap
10. stab
11. pets
12. deer
13. stop
14. won
15. time
16. golf

B.

1. ✓	2. ✗	3. ✗	4. ✓	5. ✓
6. ✗	7. ✓	8. ✗	9. ✗	10. ✓
11. ✓	12. ✗	13. ✗	14. ✓	15. ✓
16. ✗	17. ✓	18. ✗	19. ✓	20. ✗

C.

1. P	2. S	3. P	4. P	5. S
6. S	7. P	8. S	9. P	10. S
11. P	12. P	13. S	14. P	15. S
16. P	17. S	18. P	19. P	20. P

D.

word	anagram
mace	came
dias	said
ales	sale
art	tar, rat
rife	fire
cafe	face
deal	lead, dale
lamp	palm
scare	cares, races, acres
bore	robe
clean	lance
design	signed
plane	panel
stare	rates

word	anagram
miles	smile
asleep	please
stale	tales, slate, steal
earth	heart
risen	siren
snap	pans, naps, span
warder	drawer, redraw, reward
peach	cheap
drop	prod
state	teats
wasp	paws, swap
priest	stripe
prides	spider
oils	soil

TEST 4 (page 58)

Topic 19	1. w**o**rld	2. w**o**rth	3. w**a**rder	4. w**a**rts
Topic 20	5. The boy (climbed) the tree.		6. My cat (likes) cream.	
	7. Carpenters (make) things from wood.		8. Mr Douglas (closed) the door.	
Topic 21	9. end	10. pie	11. eat	12. you
Topic 22	13. one	14. two	15. two	16. one
Topic 23	17. so	18. unless	19. until	20. before
Topic 24	21–4. deal/lead; warder/reward; slate/steal; blame/amble			